NU EPPS

The Process Pro Method

A Guide to Self-Reclamation and Clarity After Burnout

PROCESS
PRO PRESS
EST 2025

Cover design, by Nu Epps.

Published by Process Pro Press.

First edition

ISBN: 979-8-218-87021-8

This book was professionally typeset on Reedsy.
Find out more at reedsy.com

I dedicate this book to my purest self.
When clarity finally found me, it felt like coming home.
This book is the fruit of that remembering—
the reward for trusting the long road back to myself.
The evidence that purpose waits patiently
for us to reclaim who we've always been.
To my purest self,
thank you for staying whole
until I was ready to return.

Contents

III THE RISE

Acknowledgments

This book reflects a journey I never took alone.

To my husband Charles, my sons Amari and Ayson, my sister Chris, my entire family, and my best friend "Roommate" - thank you for your patience, your belief, and your **love** through every high and every hard pause. You've been my anchors in storms and my fuel in seasons of stretch.

To my grandmother, Marylin Ward, your love, your presence, and your legacy live on in every page of this book. You were the first system that worked for me. I miss you. I honor you.

To every woman who's juggled vision, grief, ambition, caregiving, identity shifts, and invisible burdens while still showing up... this book is yours, too. You're not alone, and you're not crazy. You're carrying more than most people can see and still, you rise.

To my life tribe — emotional cheerleaders, prayer warriors, capital investors, business partners; co-tenants, landlords, staff; event designers, contractors, bankers, advocates, professors, volunteers, coaches, ministers, my entrepreneurial sisters, mentors, my women's empowerment community, and every client who trusted me with their chaos: thank you for allowing me to build structure alongside your stories. Your courage continues to inspire me.

And finally, to the woman reading this who's not quite sure if she's ready... I see you. I wrote this with you in mind. You are already equipped. You are already enough. Let's get aligned and let's do the work because you are deserving of the clarity you seek.

Prologue

Before the System, There Was the Silence

Every transformation begins with a moment you can no longer ignore.

For me, it wasn't a dramatic collapse or a breaking point that shouted.

It was a quiet truth spoken by someone who loved me enough to tell the truth.

"Sometimes," my husband said one night, "we just miss you."

That sentence sat heavier than any milestone I had ever achieved.

Because I had built a life that looked successful from the outside

but was quietly costing me the very people I was working so hard for.

That was the day I realized something profound:

You can build a thriving business... and still lose yourself inside of it.

You can stack accomplishments like bricks and still feel unstable.

You can automate your workflow and still feel overwhelmed.

You can structure your days and still lack clarity about why any of it matters.

The Process Pro Method™ was not born from ambition.

It was born from *awareness*.

From losing myself in systems that weren't designed for my life, my rhythm, or my womanhood.

From rebuilding a business and a self in tandem.

From deciding I no longer wanted to chase success at the cost of my peace.

This book is not a manifesto of perfection.

It's a map of becoming.

A story about alignment over achievement.

About clarity over chaos.

About the quiet courage it takes to reclaim your time, your voice, and your life.

My hope is simple:

That in these pages, you don't just learn my method -

but you find your own.

The system is nothing without the woman it serves.

And the woman is unstoppable once she understands her power.

Your clarity journey doesn't begin with a plan.

It begins with a choice.

Welcome to yours.

Introduction

Life Was Never Meant to Be This Chaotic

I wasn't always "The Process Pro."

Not long ago, I was the woman with 37 tabs open — mentally and literally. I was the one running late to everything, holding it all together with a half-charged phone, a halfway-thought-out plan, and a heart full of guilt. I was doing everything and still felt like I was failing at all of it.

By day, I was a full-time professional in middle management, managing people. By night, I was managing life. Mom. Wife. Eldest daughter. Caregiver. Dreamer. Business builder. On paper, I looked like a success story in the making. But behind the scenes, I was overwhelmed, exhausted, and quietly asking:

"How do people actually do this?"

The truth? Most people are faking it and breaking down in silence.

What nearly broke me wasn't the ambition. It was the absence of structure to support it.

So I did something radical:

I stopped trying to balance everything and started building systems for everything.

What You're Holding Is a Life Raft and a Launch Pad

This isn't just a business book. And it's not a fluffy self-help manifesto.

It's a systems manual for real life.

It's for the woman who's brilliant but buried under to-do lists.

For the mom with a business idea but no bandwidth.

For the caregiver who's also building a dream.

For the entrepreneur living in organized chaos.

For the woman who's always been "the strong one" but is finally ready to support herself with strategy.

The Process Pro Method Was Built in the Trenches

Every framework in this book was forged in real life, under real pressure.

This method wasn't born in a boardroom. It was built between daycare pickups, client calls, caregiving duties, and Google Calendar pings. I didn't have a nanny, an investor, or unlimited time. I had my faith, my family, a fierce vision, and the clarity that came from finally admitting:

I need a better way.

That better way? Systems.

But not sterile, rigid systems. Soulful ones.

Systems that don't just streamline tasks — they safeguard your peace.

That don't just make you productive — they help you breathe.

That save your time, your money, and your sanity.

You Are Not Lazy. You Are Not Disorganized. You Are Not an Imposter.

You are likely just under-supported, over-extended, and trying to build an extraordinary life without the structure to sustain it.

This book changes that.

Inside, I'll walk you through the Process Pro Method — the exact approach I used to scale my life, business, and self by using systems to create clarity, capacity, and calm. It's the same approach that powers Esyntial Elements, fuels my clients' growth, and creates space for joy in a life that once only had room for obligation.

We'll talk real strategy. Real stories. Real tools.

No fluff.

No hustle-culture hype.

No shame.

Just solutions.

By the end of this book, you'll understand how to think like a Process Pro — and more importantly, how to build like one.

Let's get into it.

I

THE UNRAVELING

This is where the mask comes off. Before we fix, we feel. These pages honor the truth behind the overwhelm - the grief, the burnout, the brilliance buried beneath survival. You'll find yourself here... because this is where we finally name what we've been carrying.

1

Becoming the Process Pro: When Life Demands a Reset

In 2012, I lost my grandmother - and with her, the delicate balance that kept my life afloat.

She wasn't just a loved one. She was our anchor. A retired matriarch with a heart full of grace and healing, she had moved from my hometown of Houston to Atlanta, where I lived with my husband, to help raise our children while we chased our professional dreams. Both of us held demanding, high impact jobs - he in corporate America, and I in higher education. At the same time, I was quietly building a boutique event consulting firm I'd founded back in 2005 after having my first son.

We had our version of balance. A rhythm. A system. Life was full but it was good.

Until it wasn't.

When her cancer returned, it came fast and cruel. Within five months, she was gone. Losing her wasn't just an emotional loss. It was an infrastructural collapse. The childcare. The peace of mind. The presence of a woman who could mother me while I was mothering everyone else. All gone.

I tried to replace her. Hired nannies. Shifted schedules. But nothing felt right. I was sick with grief. My children were heartbroken. My husband was grieving too, all while trying to meet the demands of his executive role.

And then the job I loved forced a choice.

I could keep climbing the ladder in higher education, or walk away and go home.

I chose home.

It wasn't an easy decision, but it was the right one. My two-year-old and six-year-old needed a present mother, not a burned out provider. My husband needed a partner, not a ghost. And I needed to recalibrate to build something that worked for the reality of our lives.

So I scaled up my business, poured my energy into its growth, and within two months, opened a 2,500-square-foot event space.

It felt like redemption. Rebirth. A restart.

Until it didn't.

When the Dream Becomes a Cage

I entered a business partnership that looked promising. It collapsed within 18 months. I lost resources. Lost time. Lost trust. I fell into a five day fog of depression, curled up in silence and shame.

But I'm a builder. Always have been.

So I wiped my tears, leaned on my husband, and started again...solo this time. I found a smaller space. Rebuilt my team. Threw myself into the hustle. I had vision. I had grit. I had vengeance. And I was determined to rise.

And I did...

Until I didn't.

I scaled too fast. Booked too many events. Took on too many clients. Expanded without the infrastructure to support it. The business that once gave me purpose became a pressure cooker. And when my health started to decline, everything unraveled.

I remember one event vividly - a Sweet 16 celebration that meant everything to the client and absolutely nothing to my failing body at the time. I was sick. In pain. Barely functioning. But I couldn't cancel. I couldn't fail. So I called on my tribe of entrepreneurial sisters and, through tears, asked them to show up and run the event.

Unpaid. Untrained. No questions asked.

They came. They executed. They covered for me in every conceivable way.

And I knew in that moment:

I never wanted to feel that helpless again.

Behind the Scenes of the "Boss Life"

People saw the bookings. The growth. The glam.

What they didn't see were the sacrifices.

2 a.m. installs.

The kids crying in the background while I took client calls.

The silent strain on my marriage.

The mountain of responsibilities I was juggling - HR, sales, procurement, installations, vendor management, marketing, finances, customer service and all without a blueprint.

They didn't see the guilt. The pressure. The way my home felt like a hotel I checked in and out of. The way I was over-performing as a mom to compensate for the grief ...theirs and mine. The way my husband's life seemed intact while mine quietly shattered behind the scenes.

They didn't see the debt I buried myself in, over-investing in a business without the back end systems to sustain what I was selling.

And even when things were working...

I wasn't.

I was operating on willpower alone. And my health paid the price.

Burnout Isn't Always Loud

Sometimes it looks like smiling while dying inside.

Sometimes it looks like being "booked and busy" but unfulfilled and untethered.

Sometimes it looks like success on Instagram and feels like failure in your spirit.

I had done everything "right."

But my systems were reactive, not proactive.

And when the collapse came…when my body forced me to stop - I had no choice but to start over.

This time, with intention.

The Birth of the Process Pro

My husband made the call I was too stubborn to make.

We had an estate sale. We purged everything we owned. And reluctantly - more like kicking and screaming - I relocated back to Houston.

I closed the physical doors of my business and paused operations. After starting, winning, losing, restructuring, and growing fast, I walked away from the space I had built. We moved our boys from the only home they had ever known. At my most vulnerable moment, I forced myself to communicate the transition, refund clients, and publicly bow out right at what looked like the height of my success.

I was devastated.

I had been the reason we moved in the first place. The reason we uprooted our lives. And it crushed me to leave behind what we'd built as young newlyweds.

The truth is:

I didn't just grieve my business.

I grieved my identity.

But buried in the rubble was something I hadn't expected:

Clarity.

No longer trapped in the cycle of survival, I could finally breathe…and build.

Not just a business. A blueprint.

Not just structure. A strategy.

The Process Pro was born not from perfection but from pressure.

From missteps and meltdown.

From trauma, tears, and too many tabs open.

What emerged wasn't just a method.

It was a mission.

This is the foundation. The story behind the system that made way for Nu Epps, The Process Pro to emerge.

In the next chapter, we build it together, starting with self.

2

The Breaking Point: Correcting A Self-Care Neglect System

You can't build a business that thrives...

if the person running it is drowning.

Most systems books start with time-blocking, automation, and digital tools. But that's not where my journey toward sustainable success began.

My first system wasn't a fancy app.

It wasn't a CRM.

It wasn't even a workflow template.

It was stillness.

It was the decision that I could no longer wake up in a panic, hit the ground sprinting, skip breakfast, ignore my body, and still expect my brilliance to perform on demand.

It was realizing that rest isn't a reward.

It's a requirement.

It was a decision:

I will not build a business that costs me my body.

I will not design a brand that buries my peace.

The Morning Meeting with Myself

These days, I wake up slowly... on purpose.

No jolting alarms. No urgent emails. Just soft tones that ease me into the day. I open the blinds. Let the light in. Boil water for tea.

And then I sit with myself.

Before anyone else's needs. Before the rush. Before the world gets a say.

This meeting with myself is sacred. It's where I check in with my mind, my body, my goals, my boundaries, my capacity. It's where I ask the questions that no calendar app or client portal ever will:

- What do I need today?
- How do I want to feel?
- What can wait?
- What must move forward?
- What's true for me right now?

This is where strategy begins.

A Schedule Without Self Is Just a To-Do List

Many women I work with have planners full of appointments, commitments, and color-coded obligations but not a single space carved out for themselves.

They're booked.

Busy.

Exhausted.

And still unsure if they're doing enough.

We've been taught to plan our lives around everyone else's needs. We respond to demands, fire drills, and the expectations of roles we didn't always choose - caretaker, fixer, leader, do-it-all-er.

But a system that doesn't start with **you** will eventually swallow you.

You are the engine behind the vision.

If you burn out, so does the mission.

So in the Process Pro Method, we start with what I call **Personal Systems** — the rituals, rhythms, and structures that stabilize the human behind the hustle.

Self-Care Isn't a Luxury. It's Infrastructure.

This isn't about bubble baths and spa days (though I love both).

This is about setting yourself up to operate with clarity, calm, and capacity.

Self-care, in this framework, means:

- Knowing your triggers and planning around them.
- Building buffers between meetings, calls, or high-output work.
- Creating *white space* on your calendar, as well as in your spirit.
- Protecting your mornings like they're meetings with your most important client.
- Saying **no** when the yes costs too much.

For me, self-care has looked like:

- Setting alarms that remind me to **breathe**, not just hustle.
- Drinking hot tea and journaling before the kids wake up.
- Choosing meals that nourish, not just fill.
- Ending my workday **on time**, even when there's more to do.

These aren't soft habits.

They're survival architecture.

Because if I don't protect my peace, I won't be present for the people or the purpose I'm building for.

Check Engine Lights Aren't Optional

Your body speaks before burnout does.

    That tightness in your chest.

    The Sunday night dread.

    The "I'm fine" that you know is a lie.

    You don't need to hit rock bottom to justify a reset.

    You can schedule rest before collapse.

    You can build in margin before the meltdown.

    Think of it like this:

    Your car doesn't have to catch fire before it needs gas.

    And neither do you.

The Personal Systems Audit

Here's where we begin. Take inventory - not of your tasks, but of **your tendencies**.

    Answer these questions honestly:

1. **When do I feel most clear and energized?**
2. **What time of day is hardest for me — and why?**
3. **What drains me? What nourishes me?**
4. **What do I keep saying "yes" to that no longer serves me?**
5. **Where in my day am I consistently overextended, rushed, or reactive?**
6. **What would it look like to start my day grounded — not gripped by urgency?**

This is your data. These are your patterns. And from here, we begin to build systems that support YOU and your schedule.

Self-First Isn't Selfish

When you create systems that protect your energy, your family benefits.

Your clients benefit.

Your purpose benefits.

This isn't about opting out of responsibility. It's about refusing to collapse under the weight of it.

You don't have to prove your worth through exhaustion.

You don't have to earn your rest by breaking down.

You're allowed to feel good while building something great.

Let this chapter be your permission slip.

The **system** starts with you and the **structure** starts with care.

In the next chapter, we'll move from self to strategy — and begin designing the life your systems were meant to support.

3

The Cost of Overcapacity: How Women Repeat Toxic Productivity At Home and in Business

Before you automate a funnel or outsource a task, you have to get honest about something many business owners overlook:

Your first business... is your home.

That's your first team.

Your first company culture.

Your first operations manual.

Your first leadership training ground.

And if that system is always in crisis?

Your business will reflect that chaos - even if it's dressed up in luxury branding and a packed calendar.

What I've learned over time is this:

The quality of my home systems is often the clearest indicator of my capacity to grow, serve, and lead in my business systems.

It took me years and some deep emotional excavation to figure out how to systematize my home life without losing the heart in the process.

Leadership Starts at Home

In our house, the number one system isn't tech.
It's **communication**.
We talk.
We host family meetings.
We plan ahead.
We tell the truth.
And we do it in a way that creates shared ownership.
Here's the reality:
You can't expect your business to run smoothly if your household runs on confusion, resentment, and last-minute scrambles.
So we implemented systems that allow our home to function like what it is - a living, breathing organization with values, goals, and people who matter.

The Family Meeting Framework

Once a week, we sit down together as a team - not us vs. them.
We discuss:

- **The week ahead** - who needs what, and when.
- **Meal planning** - what's on the menu, who's helping.
- **Chores** - what needs doing, and who's responsible.
- **Emotions** - what's coming up, what's weighing us down.
- **Wins** - what we're proud of, what we're celebrating.

These meetings changed our rhythm and reduced our friction.
Instead of guessing or assuming, we ask and align.
Instead of letting tasks pile up and feelings boil over, we clear the air in advance.

Delegation Isn't Just for the Office

I used to do it all at home... not because I wanted to, but because I thought I had to.

Somewhere deep inside, I believed my worth was tied to how well I managed *everything*.

But then I realized:

Delegation is a form of love.

It says: "I trust you to help carry what matters to all of us."

So now, we assign by skill, season, and strength:

- My sons rotate kitchen duty.
- My husband owns all things logistics and tech.
- I focus on planning, emotional temperature, and design flow.

No one is overfunctioning.

No one is underfunctioning.

We each play a role — and revisit those roles as life changes.

Domestic Systems Are Not Domestic Servitude

Let's be real.

Many women carry invisible labor - the mental checklists, the meal plans, the emotional tracking, the calendar syncing, the "don't forget the science fair" reminders... and still feel guilty for asking for help.

We've internalized the idea that running a home is either "natural" or "not that serious."

But systems don't strip the soul from your household.

They free it.

They allow you to love your people without resenting the weight of managing them.

They create clarity so that chaos doesn't become your family's normal.

Create Household SOPs (Yes, Really)

Think of it like business:

You wouldn't expect a new employee to succeed without on boarding, guidance, or documented processes. Why do we expect our households to magically run themselves?

Here are a few systems you can create at home:

- **Morning routine SOP** - who does what, in what order
- **Laundry system** - assigned days, folding protocol, storage zones
- **Meal planning system** - shared calendar, favorite meals list, grocery sync
- **Cleaning zones** - each person owns a space per week
- **Budget overview** - monthly financial meeting, shared access to spending goals
- **School system** - backpack checklists, homework stations, project timelines

Make it visual.

Make it collaborative.

Make it sustainable so it supports your life instead of complicating it.

When the House Runs, You Can Build the Dream

It's hard to lead powerfully at work when you're parenting reactively at home.

It's hard to close deals in your business when you're drowning in laundry and don't know what's for dinner.

You're not failing.

You're just trying to carry the weight of an empire on the back of memory and martyrdom.

Let that go.

You deserve to run your home with as much intentionality as you run your business.

Not because it needs to be perfect - but because you deserve peace.

Peace is a product of clarity.

And clarity is a product of systems.

Let your home support you.

Let it carry you.

Let it function like the living organization it is with roles, rhythms, and rest.

In the next chapter, we'll shift focus from systems that support your *life* - to the ones that support your *business*.

4

The Clarity Deficit: Why You Think You're Stuck

I didn't realize I was living the same day on repeat - until life finally demanded that I stop pretending.

There was no dramatic breakdown. No single, cataclysmic event. Just slow, quiet erosion. Subtle layers of pressure, people-pleasing, and performance wrapped themselves around my identity until I couldn't tell where my responsibilities ended and where I began.

Looking back, I see it clearly now:

My breaking point wasn't a moment.

It was a buildup.

Of unspoken truths.

Of unprocessed emotions.

Of invisible expectations.

All stacked on top of each other—until the weight of it broke through my ability to carry on.

And I did carry it.

Until I couldn't anymore.

The Night I Finally Broke Down

One night, long after everyone in the house had fallen asleep, I sat on the edge of the bed. The room was still. My hands were trembling.

Nothing had happened. And that terrified me.

I was performing. Producing. Adapting. Responding. Handling.

But inside, I felt hollow.

Exhausted in a way that sleep couldn't fix.

Foggy. Flatlined. Numb.

The scariest part?

I didn't want anything.

Not rest.

Not success.

Not escape.

Not even inspiration.

I wanted... nothing.

That was when I knew.

This wasn't about being tired.

Something deeper had shut down.

And I didn't know how to restart it.

I had become the woman everyone praised for being strong - until I couldn't be strong anymore. But I didn't tell anyone that.

I just sat there in the dark, whispering a question to myself I was too ashamed to ask out loud:

"How did I get here?"

The Day It Shifted at Work

There was a meeting at work...a moment that still sits in my chest like a bruise.

I walked in expecting collaboration. I walked out feeling like a scapegoat.

My ideas, my leadership, my loyalty - suddenly under scrutiny. What began as subtle discomfort turned into overt dismissal. People I had poured into stood silent. People I trusted avoided eye contact. The room shifted.

It wasn't just politics. It was betrayal.

And through it all, I stayed "professional."

Still performing excellence.

Still holding it together.

Still trying to prove I was enough.

I didn't know it then, but grief was shaping me.

Because loss doesn't always look like death.

Sometimes, it looks like losing yourself in a place where you once felt purpose.

The Numbness at Home

At home, I moved through life like a shadow.

Dinner.

Homework.

Errands.

Emails.

A quick scroll.

A tired smile.

A quiet "I'm fine."

But I wasn't fine. I was present, but disconnected - watching life happen from behind a glass wall.

Depression doesn't always look like sadness.

Sometimes, especially in high-achieving women, it looks like competence.

You still show up.

Still produce.

Still carry everyone else.

And yet inside, you are unraveling quietly.

You don't cry for help.

You overfunction.

The Laptop Breakdown

One day, I sat at my laptop…my safe space, my idea zone, my creative sanctuary.

And… nothing.

No spark.

No plan.

No thought.

Not procrastination. Not fear. Just a kind of **mental paralysis** that was terrifying.

This wasn't laziness. It was overload.

My brain had shut down. My creativity, the very thing that had always saved me, was suddenly inaccessible.

That's when I learned something that changed everything:

Clarity is not born from pressure.

It's born from alignment.

The Invisible Toll

Grief had rewired my brain.

Failure had bruised my self-trust.

Burnout had numbed my creativity.

Depression had fogged my clarity.

And yet I kept pushing.

Because that's what we're taught to do, right?

High-achieving women don't crumble.

We carry more.

We perform harder.

We silence our needs and overdeliver.

We don't burn out in flames.

We fade in silence—while still hitting deadlines.

And because we look "fine,"

no one checks on us.

Not even us.

I Wasn't Disorganized. I Was Misaligned.

For years, I told myself I was struggling because I lacked:

- Discipline
- Focus
- Motivation
- Structure

But the truth?

I wasn't undisciplined.

I was misaligned.

There's a psychological toll that comes from trying to operate at a high level while carrying emotional trauma. It fractures your clarity. It distorts decision-making. It silences your intuition.

You end up stuck in loops:

Start.

Stop.

Try again.

Blame yourself.

Start over.

And the whole time, you think *you* are the problem.

You're not.

The problem is **the clarity gap.**

The Cycle I Didn't Know I Was In

Every single moment of breakdown—

the betrayal

the burnout

the numbness

the fog
the spiral -
Was a symptom of one thing:
A clarity deficit.
Because when you don't know what you *really* need,
you keep repeating what you've always done.
You chase what's familiar - even when it hurts.
You tolerate cycles that should've ended years ago.

The Real Diagnosis

Psychologists call this cognitive overload:
When your brain is too full of emotional noise to process clearly.
But I call it the **Clarity Deficit**:

> *The invisible gap between what you* think *the problem is,*
> *and what the problem* actually *is.*

It shows up when:

- You keep starting from scratch
- You feel exhausted but still can't rest
- You keep performing, but feel hollow
- You can't finish what you start
- You're disconnected from your own brilliance
- You're in survival mode long after the crisis is over

This isn't failure.
This isn't a lack of discipline.
This is what happens when your internal clarity hasn't caught up to your external performance.

The Turning Point

My shift didn't come with a strategy. It came with a sentence.

One day, I finally said to myself:

"I'm not crazy. I'm not broken. I'm misaligned."

That was it.

That one sentence freed me.

Because once I named it, I could face it.

Once I saw it, I could shift it.

Once I acknowledged the gap, I could close it.

This wasn't a new hustle. It was a new awareness.

The First Seed of My Method

I didn't know it at the time, but that moment was the birth of the Process Pro Method™.

Not a template.

Not a formula.

But a *response* to misalignment.

My clarity didn't come from control.

It came from truth.

And this truth became my turning point:

> *When clarity and alignment are missing, chaos will recycle itself...*
> *no matter how brilliant or capable you are.*

The Bridge to What Comes Next

This chapter is the before.

The fog.

The numbness.

The system overload.

The emotional fatigue.

But the next chapter?
That's where the light comes in.
That's where you stop chasing productivity
and start choosing alignment.
That's where your system is no longer external—
it's you.
So now that you've seen the clarity deficit…
Let's close the gap.

5

The Clarity Gap: The AHA Moment You've Been Overlooking

I didn't recognize my own brilliance the first time it showed up.

To be honest, I almost missed it entirely.

It didn't arrive with applause, validation, or a neon sign.

It didn't feel triumphant or obvious.

It didn't even feel like success.

It felt like **relief**.

Quiet. Subtle. Familiar.

Like something finally clicking into place after being off by just a few degrees for years.

It was so understated, I almost dismissed it as nothing special.

But that moment?

That tiny, nearly invisible shift?

That was the **Clarity Gap** closing in my life for the first time.

And I didn't even know it.

The Moment I Saw Myself Clearly (and Almost Looked Away)

I was sitting across from a woman who trusted me.

She was overwhelmed, drowning in the same patterns I had just started climbing out of.

She wasn't asking for magic.

She wasn't even asking for answers.

She just wanted to breathe.

She was stuck.

Confused.

Exhausted.

Frustrated.

Falling behind in a life she had built with her own hands.

And I saw her.

I **felt** her.

Because she was me not long ago.

So I started walking her through the same quiet steps I had taken to pull my mind out of the fog, my goals out of chaos, and my identity out of hiding.

I wasn't coaching.

I wasn't selling.

I was just… helping.

She nodded.

She took notes.

She paused at the parts that hit too close to home.

And then something happened.

She came back the next week with results.

Not ideas.

Not intentions.

Results.

She moved differently.

She spoke with more clarity.

She saw herself with new eyes.

And then she said something simple, innocent, and pure:

"That thing you told me? It worked."
That should've been the moment I celebrated.
But my first reaction wasn't pride.
It was disbelief.
Me?
My process?
My way of doing things?
Surely not.
Surely she was just motivated.
Surely it was a coincidence.
Surely I didn't create anything of value.
And that right there?
That's the **Clarity Gap** in action.

What the Clarity Gap Really Is

The Clarity Gap is the space between who you **are** and who you **think** you are.
　　Between what you **do** and what you actually **recognize** in yourself.
　　Between your **natural genius** and your **acknowledged brilliance**.
　　Most women don't lack talent.
　　They lack **acknowledgment**.
　　Not from others,
From themselves.
　　I almost missed my own breakthrough,
　　Because I was conditioned not to see myself clearly.

The Psychology of Overlooking Your Own Brilliance

I didn't know this at the time, but what I was experiencing has a name:
　　Cognitive Blindness.
　　It's what happens when trauma, grief, failure, or constant survival-mode
distort your internal mirror.

You can see **everyone else's** brilliance.

But you can't see your own without guilt, doubt, or disbelief.

For high-achieving women - especially Black women - the mirror is even harder to trust.

Because we are taught:

• To downplay what comes naturally

• To minimize what we do easily

• To celebrate others before acknowledging ourselves

• To survive first and self-reflect later Or never "do too much," even while doing **everything**

Grief makes you question your **worth**.

Failure makes you question your **competence**.

Depression makes you question your **identity**.

So when brilliance shows up?

You assume it's an accident.

This is the **Clarity Gap**.

Not a lack of clarity.

But a lack of **recognition**.

And when you don't recognize it—

You don't **trust** it.

You don't **use** it.

You don't **protect** it.

You don't **build** from it.

You overlook what should have always been your starting point.

The Day I Realized I Was the System

One afternoon, while journaling, I wrote a sentence that stopped me mid-stroke:

"I process life through patterns."

I stared at it.

Read it again.

And again.

Then it hit me like a quiet, rising sun:

I have always created systems.

Even in chaos.

Even in grief.

Even in burnout.

Not because I wanted to…

But because my brain **needed** to organize survival into structure.

I had created:

• Checks and balances without calling them that

• Frameworks without naming them

• Processes without monetizing them

• Clarity without recognizing it

I thought I was **coping**.

But I was actually **architecting**.

I was building a methodology in the dark.

And every woman has something like this.

A wiring.

A rhythm.

A brilliance.

A way of thinking she assumes is **normal—**

because it's always been there.

You don't question what feels natural.

But that's the danger of the Clarity Gap:

When your brilliance feels normal,

you don't treat it like the gift it is.

The First Time Someone Reflected My Brilliance Back

After watching that first client transform, I started paying attention.

People kept telling me:

"You break things down differently."

"You always see the whole picture."

"You make chaos make sense."

"You explain things in a way that makes people feel safe."

"You can see the problem **and** the pattern."

"You process multiple layers at once."

"I always leave with clarity when I talk to you."

At first, I dismissed it.

People compliment your character, not your calling... right?

But then one person said something I couldn't ignore:

"Nu... you know this is a whole system, right?"

That word—**system**—hit something in me.

This wasn't luck.

This wasn't coincidence.

This wasn't just "how I think."

This was **intentional**.

Repeatable.

Transferable.

Transformational.

A methodology is born the moment someone else can replicate a result.

And I had already done that—without even realizing it.

The Psychology Behind the Aha

The Clarity Gap closes when your **reality** catches up to your **identity**.

It happens when:

• Truth becomes undeniable

• Patterns become visible

• Your inner voice gets louder than your doubts

• Someone mirrors your brilliance back to you

• You see yourself from outside yourself

• Results speak louder than your insecurity

That *aha moment* you're tempted to downplay?

It's not fluff.

It's not luck.

It's not a fluke.

It's the birthplace of your power.

Clarity doesn't show up with fireworks.

It shows up with **understanding**.

A knowing.

A shift.

A click.

That click?

That's your **compass**.

The System I Built Without Knowing It

Once I gave myself permission to believe my process was real, I retraced it.

Every cycle of survival.

Every burnout.

Every reinvention.

Every breakdown and rebuild.

They all followed the same inner blueprint.

My brain had been doing something consistent:

Breaking chaos into clarity through pattern recognition.

And when I mapped it out,

I found the roots of what would become the **Process Pro Method** (*See Appendix for Visual Process Pro Method Diagram*):

- **Mindset Clarity**
- **Movement Clarity**
- **Money Clarity**
- **Mission Clarity**

These weren't random.

They weren't guesswork.

They weren't accidents.

They were *me*.

My wiring.

My worldview.

My lived experience.

My internal technology.

I didn't learn this system.

I **became** it.

Becoming the Guide, Not the Glue

Most of my life, I thought I was "the glue."

The one who held everything together.

The fixer.

The reliable one.

The one who caught what others dropped.

The one who "figured it out."

But **glue holds structure together.**

Systems create structure.

I wasn't glue.

I was a **guide**.

And that changed everything.

I stopped centering survival.

I started centering **transformation**.

I stopped managing chaos.

I started **designing solutions**.

I stopped shrinking my brilliance.

I started **anchoring my identity in it**.

The Process Pro wasn't invented.

She was revealed.

Your Aha Moment Is the Beginning - Not the End

The Clarity Gap is where you finally see yourself with unfiltered honesty:

- Who you really are
- What you really do
- What you naturally create
- What you've always carried
- What comes alive in your mind
- What patterns you were born to recognize

And once you see it?
　　You can't unsee it.
　　The gap closes.
　　The identity clicks.
　　The alignment begins.
　　The doubt dissolves.
　　The brilliance emerges.
　　This is the moment you stop performing strength—
　　And start **walking in clarity**.
　　This is the shift from:
　　"I need to get it together."
　　to
　　"I am the togetherness."
　　This is the moment the method is born.
　　Your gifts were never missing.
　　You were just missing the **mirror**.
　　And now that you've seen it?
　　You're ready to walk in what's already been yours.

6

Designing a New Narrative

There comes a moment in every woman's life when she stops waiting for the plot to twist -

and realizes she's the one holding the pen.

For me, that moment came quietly.

Not in triumph.

Not in clarity.

Not even in confidence.

It arrived in the stillness that followed walking away from a job that had drained me, broken me, reshaped me...

and ultimately revealed me.

I didn't leave because I was defeated.

I left because the version of me who stayed was too small for the woman I was becoming.

We often think becoming is loud:

A dramatic transformation.

A bold declaration.

A visible shift.

But becoming is rarely loud.

Becoming is subtle.

Sacred.

Slow.

Sometimes painful.

Always necessary.

It happens in private conversations with yourself.

In the decisions you don't announce.

In the quiet choosing of yourself (long before you believe you deserve the choosing).

Leaving that university wasn't just a career change.

It was a spiritual pivot.

A reclamation.

A conscious exhale.

It was the moment I realized:

I'm not just in the chapter.

I am the author.

And once you know that truth -

you never read your life the same way again.

The Story I Was Living vs. The Story I Was Writing

For years, I believed life was something that happened to me.

Circumstances pulled.

People pushed.

Opportunities shifted.

Trauma rewired.

Expectations molded.

I was responding more than I was creating.

Adjusting more than I was deciding.

Surviving more than I was living.

But stepping out of the room where I was misunderstood, mishandled, and misnamed gave me back something grief and burnout had taken:

Perspective.

With distance came clarity.

With rest came truth.

With silence came identity.

I stopped seeing myself as a character reacting to conflict...
and started recognizing myself as a woman rewriting her purpose.

The Becoming Was Already Happening

What I thought was an ending
was actually the midpoint of an origin story.
The breaking wasn't my undoing.
The breaking was the beginning.
I didn't know the last twelve months were preparing me for this exact moment:

- The moment I acknowledged my brilliance
- The moment I trusted my patterns
- The moment grief became wisdom
- The moment burnout became blueprint
- The moment I realized my mind was a methodology
- The moment the Process Pro wasn't created—but revealed

I thought I was walking away because I was tired.
But I wasn't tired.
I was ready.
Ready to stop performing resilience.
Ready to stop shrinking my genius.
Ready to stop repeating the same cycles.
Ready to stop surviving stories that no longer served me.
Becoming demands we leave former versions of ourselves behind.
And I finally understood:
I wasn't losing anything.
I was returning to myself.

Honoring My Process

This chapter…
  This book…
  This body of work…
  They're not entertainment.
  They're documentation.
  They're evidence.
  They're legacy.
  I wrote through the unraveling.
  I wrote through the ache.
  I wrote the patterns I once ignored.
  I wrote the truths I once misdiagnosed.
  I wrote myself back into alignment.
  Back into clarity.
  Back into becoming.
  This isn't a story of pain.
  It's a story of awareness.
  Not a story of collapse.
  A story of emergence.
  Not a story of defeat.
  A story of design.
  This is the story of how I became a system.

The Professional Phoenix

Every woman who reinvents herself knows this truth:
  You rise the moment you realize you were never ruined.
  This chapter…this moment…is where the ashes settle,
  and the wings begin to stretch.
  For me, becoming wasn't a rebirth through destruction.
  It was a rebirth through **recognition**.
  I finally saw myself clearly.

Understood my wiring.
Trusted my brilliance.
Believed what others had seen in me all along.

- The Clarity Deficit was the problem.
- The Clarity Gap was the revelation.
- **Becoming** is the victory.

The Author I Am Now

I once lived at the mercy of other people's narratives—
Bosses.
Institutions.
Expectations.
Roles.
Responsibilities.
But I am not the woman I used to be.
Now, I write my own story:
Line by line.
Choice by choice.
Chapter by chapter.
I'm not waiting for permission.
I'm not asking for validation.
I'm not shrinking for comfort.
I'm not dimming for peace.
I'm not silencing my clarity.
I am becoming…
Loudly.
Softly.
Intentionally.
Unapologetically.
This is not the end of my story.
This is the naming of the narrator.

The Bridge to What Comes Next

This chapter is not closure.
It's coronation.
It completes the first arc of your clarity journey
and opens the door to what comes next.
Because once you realize you're the author?
The story expands.
And now that I am designing a new narrative...

- The Process Pro Method can be taught
- The alignment can be mapped
- The clarity can be built
- The mission can be lived
- The work can be shared

This is the end of my unraveling.
This is the beginning of my rise.
I am no longer explaining the story I lived through.
I am writing the one I choose to live next.
And so are you

II

THE REBUILDING

Here is where we rise from the rubble. With new language, fresh alignment, and soul-led systems. Hopefully, you'll rebuild your business approach and your sense of self. These chapters invite you to restructure from within, with clarity as your compass.

7

Rebuilding from the Rubble: What You Have is Enough to Reframe

Before there was social media.

Before apps, automations, or AI.

Before I had a CRM, a funnel, or a digital product…

I had Microsoft Outlook — and pure intention.

That was my first system.

And it changed everything.

I wasn't trying to build a "tech stack." I was just trying to stay afloat.

Trying to separate business from personal — without paying $500 a month.

Trying to look legit… when all I had was a laptop, a few leads, and more grit than tools.

So I systematized what I had.

That's what makes a Process Pro™.

Audit Before Automation

By the time I burned out (the first time), I had learned something most entrepreneurs don't realize until it's too late:

You don't just need systems to scale.

You need systems to survive.

After taking a hard look at my personal life and household (see Chapter 3), I realized the same emotional patterns that led me to say "yes" too often at home were also sabotaging my business.

People-pleasing.

Overbooking.

Undercharging.

Avoiding structure in the name of "freedom."

But freedom without structure is just floating.

And floating doesn't get you far.

So I took the same approach I used to reclaim my peace at home — and applied it to my business.

The Four Core Business Systems

(See Appendix for Four Core Business Systems Diagram)

Every business (no matter the size or industry) runs on four essential systems:

1. **Client Flow** — How people find you, book you, and experience your service
2. **Operational Flow** — How your team, tools, and time are managed
3. **Financial Flow** — How money is tracked, allocated, and optimized
4. **Marketing Flow** — How your message is shared, seen, and sustained

You may call them something else. You may combine or segment them differently. But if any one of these flows is clogged, scattered, or absent? Growth becomes grind.

Client Flow: Make It Easy to Say Yes

You should not be doing mental gymnastics every time someone asks, "How can I work with you?"

That question should have a systemized, seamless, and scalable answer.

Client Flow includes:

- Inquiry responses (automated or templated)
- Calendly or booking links with built-in buffers
- Welcome emails and on boarding steps
- Digital contracts and invoices
- Clear service menu or offer ladder
- Off boarding surveys or testimonial capture

Don't wait until you're overwhelmed to systematize this.

Make it easy for people to enter, enjoy, and exit your world professionally.

Operational Flow: You're Not a Machine

You are not your admin assistant, tech department, sales rep, and janitor all in one.

You might be wearing all the hats today, but systems ensure you don't wear them forever.

Operational Flow includes:

- Task management (Asana, ClickUp, Trello)
- Weekly CEO meeting with yourself (or your team)
- SOPs for recurring tasks (yes, even small ones)
- A documented file structure (Google Drive, Dropbox, etc.)
- Password management systems (like LastPass or 1Password)
- Team roles and communication channels (Slack, Voxer, email protocols)

If it lives only in your head, it's not a system. It's a liability.

Financial Flow: Numbers Don't Lie

Avoidance doesn't protect your peace. It postpones your power.
Financial Flow includes:

- Invoicing and payment tracking
- Weekly or bi-weekly financial check-ins
- Expense categorization
- Profit-first allocation (e.g., owner's pay, taxes, ops)
- Bookkeeping systems or software (QuickBooks, Wave, etc.)
- Income goal tracking

You can't scale what you won't look at.
Clarity here is about responsibility.
And financial responsibility is one of the greatest forms of self-respect in business.

Marketing Flow: Say It Once, Use It Twice

You don't have to create new content every day.
You need a system to **repurpose, recycle, and reframe** what you already know.
Marketing Flow includes:

- Core brand messaging doc (your values, voice, vision)
- Social media templates and themes
- Email marketing schedule
- Content bank (past posts, testimonials, etc.)
- Launch calendars and promotional timelines
- Analytics tracking (what's working, what's not)

When your marketing has a rhythm, you no longer chase visibility - you attract it with intention.

You Don't Need Fancy Tools. You Need Functional Flow.

Some of the most organized, profitable entrepreneurs I know use:

- Google Calendar
- Spreadsheets
- Voice notes
- Boundaries

Don't let tech shame or comparison culture keep you stuck.
A Process Pro uses what she has and optimizes it as she grows.
Start with clarity.
Then build consistency.
Then, and only then, layer on complexity.

Scaling Shouldn't Cost Your Sanity

Yes, your business matters.
Yes, your clients matter.
Yes, your vision matters.
But **you** matter more.
There is no version of success worth sacrificing your sleep, health, family, or identity.
So build with systems.
Build with foresight.
Build with care.
In the next chapter, we'll talk about how to build for the long haul without burning out, breaking down, or backing out.
You've got the structure.
Now let's talk about staying power.

8

The Alignment Awakening: Understanding Your Systems and Capacity

When most people talk about scaling, they immediately jump to money.

More clients.

More leads.

More products.

More platforms.

But in my world?

The first thing I scaled... was time.

Because when you're stretched to your limits, time becomes your currency.

And when you finally get clear on who you are, how you want to work, and what kind of life you're no longer willing to tolerate - the systems you build don't just make life easier...

They give you back the capacity to think.

And that changed everything.

From Burnout to Blueprint

After I closed my event space in Atlanta and relocated to Houston, I was emotionally and financially bruised. However, I wasn't broken.

I had done the work.

I'd healed from the crash.

And for the first time in years, I could breathe.

Because I wasn't running from fire to fire.

The systems I'd built in Atlanta - the workflows, the routines, the automation all followed me. But everything felt different now. I wasn't hustling for survival. I was building from clarity.

I had no physical location, no showroom, and no team.

But I had peace.

And I had a plan.

I started working from home, offering virtual consulting for solopreneurs and service providers who were brilliant but buried in chaos. I took my hard-won lessons and turned them into tools. I created packages. Built workflows. Launched digital offers.

And most importantly:

I structured my business to fit my life — not the other way around.

Clarity Is the Shortcut You've Been Avoiding

Before I scaled again, I got painfully honest about three things:

1. **What do I want to build — really?**
2. **What does it cost me to build that — emotionally, energetically, financially?**
3. **What do I refuse to sacrifice again?**

Those answers became my blueprint.

They gave me the freedom to:

- Say no without guilt
- Set capacity-based boundaries
- Package my brilliance in ways that didn't rely on my constant presence
- Automate without detachment
- Rest without shame

Growth isn't always about expansion.
Sometimes it's about **refinement**.

What I Stopped Doing

Let me tell you what growth looked like for me:

- I stopped trying to offer everything to everyone.
- I stopped reinventing the wheel with every new client.
- I stopped over-customizing to prove my value.
- I stopped chasing revenue at the cost of rest.
- I stopped building alone.

These weren't just business decisions.
They were boundary decisions.
And they gave me something I hadn't had in years:
Margin.

What I Started Doing

With the systems now running and the clutter cleared, I began:

- Productizing my services into repeatable offers
- Automating lead capture and onboarding
- Hiring support — not just out of desperation, but with intention
- Blocking time for strategy, not just service
- Protecting my energy like it was a business asset (because it is)

That margin bought me more than time.

It bought me creativity.

Vision.

Joy.

Presence with my family.

Room to breathe.

And that's when I realized:

Scaling isn't about adding more.

It's about removing what no longer serves.

The Growth Systems Audit

Before you go chasing new tools or bigger platforms, pause and ask yourself:

- What am I currently doing that could be documented, delegated, or deleted?
- What systems are missing — and what's that costing me?
- What's working so well I've stopped noticing it?
- Where am I leaking time, energy, or money?
- What do I want more of — and what needs to shift to make room for it?

Growth doesn't require burnout.

But it does require truth.

Give Yourself Back to Yourself

At one point in my life, I gave everything to everyone... except me.

And the systems I teach today aren't just about getting organized or building empires.

They're about **liberation**.

The kind of liberation that gives you your time back.

Your joy back.

Your clarity back.

Your **self** back.

Because when your systems are aligned with your values and your vision? Growth becomes grace-filled.

Sustainable.

And deeply satisfying.

In the next chapter, we'll bring it all together and outline how to stay in motion, even when life shifts again. Because it will.

But this time, you'll be ready.

9

Your Story Is Your Strategy

My Story: Scaling Self to Scale Life

When we relocated to Texas, I took a full-time role at a major university. I was healing — physically, mentally, and emotionally. The salary was steady, but more than that, it bought me something priceless:

Time.

Time to think. Time to build. Time to reimagine how I wanted to work for myself.

In the margins of that 9–5, I began to quietly rebuild.

I hosted *Process Pro* workshops on weekends.

Led *Stilettos & Strategies* events each year.

And slowly, I began to rebuild what I had left behind in Atlanta - but this time, with alignment.

No rush. No pressure.

Eventually, I left the job.

Scaled *Esyntial Elements*.

Celebrated my son's first year of college.

Supported my youngest through his milestones.

Earned my MBA.

Watched my husband thrive through the most successful years of his career.

And all the while, I ran a thriving business
on my own terms.
This is what scaling clarity looks like ...
When *peace*, *pace*, and *purpose* become the byproducts of the plan.

Rebuilding the Brand — The Cost of Clarity

Leaving Atlanta wasn't just closing the doors of a business.
It was walking away from a version of myself that was wildly successful, deeply exhausted, and entirely unsustainable.
Relocating to Texas wasn't glamorous. It was gut-wrenching.
We left a three-story home, a thriving business, and our well-worn rhythm...
for two bedrooms in my in-laws' house.
Our essentials tucked into closets and a storage unit.
Technically, we were homeless.
But we were covered in love.
What many didn't know:
We moved because I was sick.
Really sick.
And figuring out *why* was expensive.
My husband made the hard but loving decision to get me the care I needed.
That meant giving up everything we had built.
It meant taking contracts that pulled him across the globe — to the Philippines, to Colombia —
while I underwent surgery, healing, and a slow rebuild of my physical, emotional, and financial self.

The Unseen Costs

It cost us space.
It cost us comfort.
It cost me pride.

But what we gained was equally invaluable:

- Support
- Humility
- Patience
- And a quiet kind of resilience that only forms when you're rebuilding with faith and no blueprint

My oldest son struggled the most.

Fifth grade was replaced with unfamiliarity, isolation, and hard truths about what it means to start over.

My youngest - in kindergarten - adjusted beautifully.

And as a family, we held tight to our values and to each other.

Our rituals shifted.

But our bond? Unshaken.

The structure was softer... no GroupMe just yet but the essence of our unity remained.

And in the midst of it all, I reopened an office.

A small, familiar corner that felt like home.

The Mini Comeback

My husband, wise as ever, gave me the green light to feel whole again.

And for me, that meant starting small.

I hosted *Process Pro* pop-up workshops.

Led mastermind intensives.

Served clients - one Saturday at a time while still healing, still learning, still grieving.

Then came the invitation.

A sorority sister mentioned a new department at a major university.

They needed someone to build operations from the ground up.

I said yes.

One month later, I was back in higher education —

and within five years, I'd earned two promotions, launched multiple initiatives, and finally said yes to something I'd long put off: **graduate school.**

During the height of the pandemic, while my oldest graduated high school

-

I graduated with my MBA in Organizational Change Management.
Poetic, isn't it?

The girl who had burned out running a quarter-million-dollar business with no systems…

was now professionally certified in exactly what once broke her.

Shifting the Model

Texas was different.

The event industry wasn't Atlanta.

It wasn't opulent. It wasn't fast-paced. It wasn't buzzing.

And neither was I.

The *Process Pro Method*™ had already begun to crystalize through my coaching work -

but now it had to become a business model.

Event planning gave way to project management.

Trade shows, vendor teams, and operations consulting became the new norm.

Gone were the massive teams, the overhead costs, the 2 a.m. chaos.

I had learned to scale the *way* I worked -

and the *type* of work I was called to do.

Quietly, *Esyntial Elements Consulting* was reborn — with a new mission.

What began as a part-time wedding hustle…

became a full-service management firm.

And that firm?

Evolved into a boutique operations consultancy that now made space for my coaching, my clarity, and my calling.

I said goodbye to my university role eight years later —

and walked fully back into entrepreneurship… again.

But this time, with the most clarity I had ever had.

Lean Into Your Story

If you've made it this far, you already know…
this book isn't about me.
It's about *you*.
The version of you ready to trade burnout for beach sides.
Overwhelm for organization.
And chaos… for clarity.
But before you rewrite your offer or rebrand your business plan, I want you to pause.
Because what if the strategy you're looking for isn't a new certification, a funnel, or a business idea?
What if it's already inside your story?

The Myth of "Starting Over"

After I shut down my event business and left Atlanta, I had a choice:
Shrink.
Or shift.
And as I sat with everything I thought I had lost -
the building, the clients, the buzz, the brand -
I realized something powerful:
I hadn't lost my strategy.
I had *lived* it.
The late nights. The launches. The lessons. The collapses. The comebacks.
They weren't separate from the work.
They were the work.
They were the *curriculum.*
So instead of starting over…
I started to lead with the truth.

Let People See You

I began telling the story.
  Not the polished version.
  The *process* version.
  The hard parts.
  The real parts.

- The "I couldn't afford the subscription fee, so I bought the leads one at a time" part.
- The "I designed my back end with free tools" part.
- The "I wore myself into illness and had to choose healing" part.

And do you know what happened?
  People leaned in.
  Not out of pity — but recognition.
  They saw *themselves*.
  And in seeing themselves, they saw *hope*.
  That's when I realized something profound:
  Your transparency is not a weakness.
  It's a shortcut to trust.
  And trust?
  Is the ultimate conversion tool.

Your Lived Experience Is Your Intellectual Property

You don't need to be famous.
  You don't need 10,000 followers.
  You don't need a perfect funnel.
  What you *do* need is:

- A clear point of view
- A lived experience that shaped your approach

- A repeatable method (even if it's still evolving)
- The courage to say:
- **"This is what I've learned. I can help you."**

That's what *Process Pro*™ became for me.

And that's what *you* can build, too.

You won't create a copy of my method, but you *will* create a container for your own, using my proven process tools.

Whether you're:

- A creative finally ready to structure your gifts
- A coach tired of winging it
- A professional ready to monetize what comes naturally
- Or a woman rebuilding after a reset...

You already have the raw material.

Your job now is to refine it...

into something that serves others *while sustaining you.*

10

The Process Pro Method™: Turning Chaos into Clarity + Strategy into Systems

By the time I finished rebuilding my life, my business, and my capacity, I realized something important:

I hadn't just recovered.

I had designed a *new* way to lead.

What started as personal survival had become professional strategy.

What once felt like failure had become the foundation.

And what I know now with certainty is this:

> *Structure creates space for freedom.*
> *Systems create room for growth.*
> *And clarity? Clarity is the spark that ignites it all.*

That's why I created the **Process Pro Method™**.

It's not a productivity hack.

It's my testimony.

It's a practical strategy for high-capacity women who are done performing, over-functioning, and living inside someone else's definition of success.

The Three Pillars of the Process Pro Method™

Each pillar reflects a transformation I lived through and now lead others through. (*See Appendix for Visual Model)*

1. Clarity First

Who are you beyond the title, the trauma, and the to-do list?
Before you build the website.
Before you plan the launch.
Before you sell a single thing...
You need **clarity**.
Ask yourself:

- What do I want?
- What do I believe?
- What is no longer sustainable?
- What is my *current* vision?
- Who am I without the building, the team, or the platform?

Most people skip this visioning stage and then wonder why the systems they bought don't work.
They're building for someone they haven't even defined.
Clarity helped me detach from reputation, release performance pressure, and rebuild based on my *truth*, not the trauma of "losing it all."

2. Systems That Sustain

What are you repeating that can be **automated, delegated, or simplified**?
Once I reclaimed time and peace at home, I saw how many parts of my business were still held together by **charisma and exhaustion**.
That's when I applied system thinking to every area:

- **Client inquiries**: Automated replies and workflows
- **Finances**: QuickBooks replaced the janky spreadsheets
- **Scheduling**: Buffered calendar blocks + automated reminders
- **Delivery**: Dubsado, email sequences, and pre-built templates
- **Space-sharing**: Virtual offices and auto-tours

You don't need to be techy.

You need to be clear.

I started with **Outlook** and **MagicJack**.

You can start with your inbox and your boundaries.

3. Strategy in Every Sector

Once clarity and systems are in place, your **business model must match the life you want**.

I no longer build offers out of panic.

I don't scale just because I can.

Every offer I've created since moving to Houston has been intentional, not reactionary.

That's how I restructured my business into three aligned sectors that serve my clients, my community, and my own vision… without draining me.

The Process Pro Ecosystem™

When I returned to events, everything was different.

No more massive teams.

No more late nights doing it all myself.

No more high overhead.

Instead, I transitioned to:

- Production-style events
- Trade shows
- Vendor coordination

Projects that allowed me to use my **brain**, not just my **body**.

The result?

I protected my energy, kept my income stable, and gained back my peace.

I realized this was not just possible. It was *scalable, smart,* and *sustainable.*

The Epiphany: I Didn't Need to Duplicate. I Needed to Evolve.

Houston wasn't Atlanta.

And I wasn't the same woman who left.

And that was okay.

I wasn't recreating the old version of life.

I was *rebuilding a new one.*

That shift gave birth to the Process Pro Ecosystem:

✳ **Nu Epps: The Expert & Brand**

This is the **personal brand** — the face, the voice, the thought leadership. Here's where I lead through:

- **Storytelling** — My journey *sells* my strategy.
- **Merch** — Not just fashion, but wearable affirmation:
- "Clarity is the New Currency"
- "Process Pro Certified"
- "Strategy Over Hustle"
- "Build Wealth, Not Followers"
- **Speaking** — Keynotes, panels, and podcasts that empower others to do the deep work
- **Licensing** — Tools and frameworks that allow other coaches and consultants to implement my systems with their own clients

Nu is the anchor.

She breathes life into everything else.

✳ **Esyntial Elements: The Operations Engine**

This is where the **real work** happens.

Esyntial Elements is my consulting and implementation firm. We specialize in:

- Business audits and clarity mapping
- Workflow & automation
- SOP development
- Onboarding frameworks
- Done-for-you launch systems

Some clients come for strategy.

Others want us to *build the whole system.*

When you don't have time to think?

We do the thinking for you.

✳ Stilettos & Strategies: The Sisterhood

This is the **bridge** — the heartbeat of the ecosystem.

Not a coaching program. Not a funnel.

A **community** — built for capacity and connection at *every* stage of business.

Here's what makes us different:

- No judgment if you're in startup… or scale-up… or "I need a break" mode
- Intentional events, not random brunches
- Real accountability paired with real empathy
- We normalize *clarity*, not *chaos*

This is where women **witness** each other:

Aspiring.

Building.

Pivoting.

Leading.

Living.

It's where business becomes legacy — in *community*.

Alignment Was the Strategy All Along

Every time I lost something — a building, a partnership, a dream —
I got clearer.
And every time I got clearer:

- My systems got simpler
- My services got sharper
- My offers got lighter
- My life got better

This ecosystem didn't just *happen*.
I designed it.
With clarity.
With intention.
With grace.
And if you're reading this thinking,
"I've lost so much, I don't even know where to begin..."
Let me tell you this:

> *Start with what's true.*
> *Then build what's yours.*
> *The systems will follow.*

11

The Internal Audit: When the System Breaks, Begin Within

Before systems saved me,

I had to save myself from the inside out.

No one talks about the heartbreak of building something that *works*, but quietly wounds you in the process.

When I lost the structure that held my life together — my grandmother — my equilibrium shattered.

My clarity scattered.

I scrambled to replace that internal support with strategy.

And while the systems I built offered relief…

> **They did not heal the parts of me that were grieving, tired, resentful, or afraid to ask for help.**

The Hidden Phase of Entrepreneurship

There's a stage no one talks about:
  The *pause*.
  The ugly cry.
  The bathroom-floor moment when you wonder if all your effort meant anything.

What Systems Can't Do

They cannot fix what you refuse to face.
  They cannot regulate your nervous system.
  They cannot unlearn toxic productivity.
  They cannot love you through a breakdown.
  Before I ever taught others how to audit their business, I had to audit myself.
  I had to sit with the hard questions:

- What is driving me?
- Why am I afraid to slow down?
- Who am I still trying to prove something to?

That's where the **Process Pro Method**™ *truly* began.
  Not in automation.
  But in *awareness. (See Internal Audit Loop Framework in Appendix)*

The Emotional Intake: Honoring Your Season

When I work with high-performing women, we don't start with workflows.
  We don't jump into software or strategy.
  We start with **emotional intake**.

  What season are you in?
    Healing? Building? Breaking? Resting? Expanding?

73

Because no system will work if it doesn't honor the *season you're in*.

Reflection Prompts

Try these before you reach for your next tool:

- What part of your story have you tried to *organize* before you've truly *processed* it?
- What emotion is driving urgency in your business that should be unpacked?

You must make peace with this truth:

> **Your first system is you.**
> *And if your beliefs are chaotic, no spreadsheet will save you.*

When the System Breaks — Rebuilding in Real Time

Moving to Texas wasn't some dream relocation.

It was survival.

Medical issues hit our household hard.

Two entrepreneurs, suddenly faced with costs that offered no corporate cushion.

The weight of what we left behind in Georgia...

a three-story home, a full-scale event venue, a life we built from scratch pressed on me harder than I let anyone see.

We moved into two bedrooms in my in-laws' house.

Our essentials packed into closets and a storage unit.

I was healing - physically, emotionally, spiritually.

From surgery.

From loss.

From ego.

My husband stepped in to provide more - traveling long stints in Colombia and the Philippines.

My in-laws, gracious and grounding, gave me space to rest and reset.

But here's the tension no one talks about:

What happens when you go from **CEO of your life** to a **guest in someone else's home?**

I wasn't resentful.

I was just... *lost.*

I missed the autonomy.

The spark.

The rhythm.

So, on our first full day in Texas, my husband gave me permission and support to build again...

just something small.

I opened a one-room coaching suite.

I hosted weekend intensives.

And slowly, I started to breathe again.

I was still healing.

But I was moving.

The Unlearning

We cannot become who we're meant to be...

without shedding who we *thought* we had to be.

There's deep power in **release...**

The kind that isn't quitting, but choosing differently.

Unlearning looks like:

- Forgiving yourself for what you didn't know
- Releasing loyalty to over-functioning
- Accepting that even your failures are *feedback*
- Realizing capacity isn't weakness - it's clarity

My Grandmother Was My First System

She had no degrees.
   No wealth.
   No blueprint.
   But her **presence was a process**.
   She showed up with love, discipline, and resourcefulness.
   She mothered me into strategy long before I knew what to call it.
   She made me laugh.
   She taught me not to take everything so seriously.
   I still hear her voice:

> *"Baby girl, if you're bald with one strand of hair, keep it clean and curled.*
> *And if you've got one tooth — make it sparkle."*

She visits me often, especially when a client says:
   "I'm not where I need to be."
   I smile like she would,
   and say simply:

> *"That's OK.*
> *We're going to make what you* do *have sparkle."*

Even in her absence, she speaks.
   Every time I resist perfection and lean into *process*, I hear her:

> *"Baby girl, keep living.*
> *Things will work out just fine.*
> *I never worry. I don't stress.*
> *And I've never cared what anybody thinks as long as I'm being true to*
> *myself and my family."*

We Are Our Own Alchemists

We are the product of process.
   The fruit of resilience.
   The legacy of women who built homes, healed wounds, fed dreams, and made something out of almost nothing.
   Our becoming is both **messy** and **divine**
   Because of the women who came before us
   and the ones we are still becoming.

Reflection Prompts

- What belief must you unlearn in order to become who you are becoming?
- What process are you judging when you should be *revering* it?

And while it may feel uncomfortable to look inward, it's there in the quiet examination of your own rhythm that you'll find what truly needs to shift. Because when you realign your inner systems, your outer success begins to follow. This is not just about fixing what's broken. It's about finally honoring what you've outgrown.

III

THE RISE

You've embraced your truth. You've reclaimed your time. Now it's time to walk fully in your power. This final section is your reminder that you don't have to shrink, strive, or settle to live the life you desire. You do not have to become...you already are.

12

Time Is the Currency. Clarity Is the Return.

Time Is the Currency. Clarity Is the Return.

I used to run my life like a 24/7 pop-up shop:
Always open.
Always available.
Always sold out.
It worked…until it didn't.
Until the profit came at the expense of peace.
Until my systems worked for the business but *not* for the woman behind it.

The Wake-Up Call

There was a day my husband sat me down. Gently. Quietly. With a truth I wasn't ready for.

> *"You put so much value on building your business," he said, "but it's starting to feel like you're downplaying everything I carry to keep us afloat. Me and the boys... we're tired. We're tired of every moment with*

you being consumed by business. Sometimes we just want you."

He said he was tired of going to weddings alone.

Tired of making appearances solo.

Tired of people asking if we were still together because no one ever saw me anymore.

He wasn't angry. He was honest.

And in that moment, I saw myself or rather, the *absence* of myself — through his eyes.

I had built something that looked successful on the outside

but was quietly wounding the people I loved most on the inside.

I had created a structure that forced me to choose between *staying afloat* and *staying connected*.

That was the moment everything changed.

The Time Wealth Shift

I began to ask myself a new kind of question:

> **If I had to buy back my time,**
> **what would it cost me to reclaim my peace?**
> **My presence?**
> **My people?**

I started treating time like **money**.

I gave every hour a **job**, a **boundary**, and a **purpose**.

I budgeted my **energy** the way I once obsessed over cash flow.

But this wasn't just about better planning.

It was about deeper *truth-telling*.

Time became **sacred.**

I built in white space.

I added decompression blocks after heavy work.

I stopped stacking sessions back-to-back.

And I gave my family **recurring calendar time** - a non-negotiable.
Because if my systems only honored my success but not my softness,
then they were broken by design.

Time, Ego, and the False Beliefs We Swallow

Part of what I had to face was **ego**.

Not arrogance but the quiet, hungry belief that my worth was tied to how much I produced.

To how many clients I served.

To how many hours I stayed "on."

I also had to confront the **patriarchal pace of productivity** I had unconsciously inherited.

The success systems we're often sold weren't built for women...

especially not for women who mother, who manage households, who hold emotional labor.

My grandmother understood this.

She never chased hustle.

But her process was steady.

Sacred.

Feminine.

True.

She held space in a way that wasn't loud, but powerful.

And in her absence, I found myself grieving not just her

but the *way* she made life make sense.

She knew something I hadn't yet learned:

> **Femininity is a system.**
> **Nurturing is a strategy.**
> **Rest is a resource.**

Coaching Tool: Time Integrity Audit

Here's one of the most confronting and transformative tools I use with clients:

1. List your **top 3 life values**
2. Audit your last 7 **days in 30-minute increments**
3. **Color-code** the time blocks that *honored* those values

Most people are shocked at how little of their time actually reflects what they *say* matters most.

Client Story: Tamia

Tamia was a program director and startup coach.
High capacity. High impact. High anxiety.
After a time audit, she discovered that **60% of her week was reactive**:
urgent client fixes, back-to-back DMs, fire drills masked as requests.
We created time blocks.
Implemented a personal "3-day response rule."
Established actual space to breathe.
In less than two months:

- Her anxiety was cut in half
- Her program doubled in capacity
- Her calendar finally honored *her*

The Mindset Layer

Here's what most productivity gurus miss:

Time management is emotional management.

Your schedule is not just a to-do list.

It's a mirror.
It reflects your *boundaries*, your *beliefs*, and your *burdens*.
When you begin to see your calendar as a *truth-teller*,
you also begin to reclaim your power.

Quick Reflection Exercise

Imagine you could only work **10 hours a week**:

- What would you keep?
- What would you cut?
- What parts of your business are draining your time
- but offering no clarity or return?

And deeper still:
    What emotional reward are you chasing by staying busy?

What Time Wealth Really Buys

As I stepped away from the hustle,
    I finally found something richer than money:
    Margin.
    Time to cook slowly.
    Time to be present without multitasking.
    Time to grieve, to laugh, to wander.
    Time to choose *rest* without guilt.
    And in that margin, I found clarity again.
    I had spent so long squeezing more out of my day...
    trying to prove that I was worthy, capable, indispensable.
    Now?

> *I demand **less** of myself*
> *So I can honor **more** of my life.*

85

That's when I knew I had discovered a new currency.

Not Bitcoin.

Not brand deals.

Not busy badges.

But clarity.

And that's the kind of wealth I intend to keep.

The way you spend your time reveals what you believe about your future. When clarity leads, time stops slipping through the cracks. You move with precision. You choose with power. You begin to live like your time is sacred... because it is.

13

Case Studies in Clarity: The Women Who Built Their Way Back

Case Studies in Clarity

Let's go deeper.

It's one thing to talk about transformation.

It's another to *witness* it.

These are real women. Real businesses. Real breakthroughs.

Each one brave enough to **systematize their peace** — and powerful enough to lead from clarity.

Client 1: The Overwhelmed CEO — "Keisha"

The Problem:

Keisha was running a growing business entirely by hand juggling manual emails, contracts, follow-ups, scheduling, and client on boarding. She was missing milestones, stuck in the weeds, and had zero capacity to scale.

Systems Applied:

- Mapped her full client journey

- Built a Dubsado onboarding workflow (email, contracts, follow-ups)
- Integrated seamless calendar booking

Mindset Shift:

> *Letting go of control isn't loss.*
> *It's **transformational leadership**.*

Results:

Keisha saved 10–12 hours a week.

She redirected that time toward visibility and marketing.

She on boarded 3 new clients without a single Zoom call.

Client 2: The Avoidant Creative — "Brandi"

The Problem:

Brandi believed structure would kill her creativity.

In reality, *avoiding structure* was killing her growth.

She resisted systems because she feared they would feel like cages.

Systems Applied:

- Designed time blocks with *freedom zones*
- Integrated HoneyBook for proposals and invoicing
- Built a templated content calendar in Airtable

Soft Skill Taught:

> *Accountability via* creative boundaries.
> *Redefining structure as* support, *not restriction*.

Results:

Brandi launched a full digital product suite.

Her income grew from $2K to $9K/month in just three months.

Her creativity finally had a *container* and it flourished.

Client 3: The Silent Drowner — *"Nicole"*

The Problem:

Nicole looked like she had it all together.

But behind the scenes, she was drowning in **invisible labor** - home, family, business... with no room to breathe.

Systems Applied:

- Created a CEO Day routine
- Audited and delegated personal responsibilities
- Launched a family communication system (GroupMe + shared calendar)

Emotional Work:

Naming the cost of silence.
Making room *for rest.*

Results:

Nicole enrolled in therapy.

She hired a virtual assistant.

She added **"joy hours"** to her weekly schedule - guilt-free.

Your Process Pro™ Takeaway

The system only works when it matches your story.

You can't borrow someone else's blueprint.

You must build your own based on your **energy**, your **bandwidth**, your **truth**.

These case studies don't just show you the power of systems.

They show you the **possibility** of designing your life *on purpose.*

Reflection Prompt:

- Which client did you relate to most — Keisha, Brandi, or Nicole?
- What part of *their* process is yours to try on?
- Where in your life are you resisting structure when it could actually set you free?

The Feminine System Framework

(See Visual Framework in Appendix)

For generations, we were taught that **masculine hustle** was the gold standard of success:

- Rigid hours
- Emotionless leadership
- Constant, unquestioned output

But as women, our genius lives in nuance, nurturing, intuition, and creative leadership.

We bring life to what we touch - including systems.

Here's how I define the **Process Pro™ Feminine System Framework**:

CRM = Community Relational Magnetism

Our nurturing presence draws people in.

It builds trust, creates loyalty, and sustains long-term connection.

We don't just close sales, we cultivate *community*.

Spiritual Intelligence

Our intuition is **data**.

We sense what others overlook.

We solve from logic and from *soul*.

Maternal Instincts = Community Building

Whether you're a parent or not, you carry life-giving energy:
Ideas. Teams. Businesses. Safe spaces.
We build *ecosystems*, not just empires.

Alluring Delivery

Our leadership is soft but potent.
Our systems are beautiful, not just functional.
Our storytelling is magnetic.
Our strategies do not intimidate.
Being a Process Pro™ doesn't mean shrinking to fit into a masculine mold.
It means embodying your **full feminine brilliance**
and honoring your *natural rhythm* as a leader, creator, and woman.

The Invitation

You don't have to choose between logic and softness.
You don't have to sacrifice success to live gently.
You don't have to "man up" to build your vision.
You just have to build systems that reflect your **truth** and not your trauma.

14

Your Clarity Journey: The Blueprint, The Build-Out, The Back End Support

You've seen the systems.

You've felt the story.

Now it's time to start *your own*.

The Process Pro Method™ isn't a template.

It's a trajectory. It is a layered, living journey of **alignment, clarity, and execution**.

And like every transformation worth taking…

It begins with **choice**.

The Process Pro Journey Map

A High-Level Framework (See Appendix for Visual Model)

Here is the simplified model that outlines the path many of my clients and I have walked.

It isn't rigid. It's real.

And it meets you where you are.

Awareness

Recognize the chaos, burnout, or misalignment you've been pushing through.

Audit

Evaluate your time, energy, tools, offers, boundaries, and beliefs.

Alignment

Recalibrate your goals based on the *woman you are now*, not the one you used to be.

Activation/Adjustment

Apply the right systems, tools, workflows, and boundaries. Delegate where needed. Automate what drains. Life shifts — so should your systems. Reassess your season, your capacity, and your priorities.

Ascension

Step into your next level with confidence, clarity, and CEO-level strategy that honors your *wholeness*.

This is the roadmap.

But the **journey?** That part is yours to walk.

This Is Not the End.

It's the Blueprint.

If you take nothing else from this book, let it be this:

✦ *You are not disorganized.*

- ✦ *You are not an imposter.*
- ✦ *You are not too late.*

You are simply **unstructured** and **structure can be built**.
Start messy.
Start small.
Start scared if you must.
But *start with strategy*.
And let that strategy flow from your story.

- Build a system that honors your rhythm.
- Design a life that doesn't burn you out.
- Lead in a way that lets you *breathe, create,* and *thrive*.

You are not broken.
You are in process.
And your process is powerful.

Final Reflection Exercise

Use these to shape your next 90 days:

1. What's the clearest lesson your life has taught you?
2. What system do you need most right now?
3. Where are you out of alignment in your business or career model?
4. What tasks or expectations do you need to automate, delegate, or delete?
5. What would **ease** feel like in your next season?

Use your answers not as tasks...
But as permission slips *to build the life you were born to lead.*

Your Story Is Strategy.

Your System Is Sacred.
   Your Process Is Your Power.
   Thank you for letting me walk this road with you.
   Thank you for seeing me and for allowing yourself to be seen.
   Thank you for being bold enough to *seek clarity*...
   And brave enough to *sustain it*.
   You are the Process Pro™ now.

Let's build legacies. Together.

> *This is not just a conclusion. This is your inflection point. A blueprint in your hands. A choice at your feet. You don't need more motivation. You need momentum and that begins with the very next decision. Let clarity be your compass now. The journey has already begun.*

What Comes Next?

You've got the blueprint.
   You can take this method and run with it. That alone makes me proud.
   But if you're ready for *more*:
   Deeper support, personalized structure, done-with-you strategy —
   I'm here when you are.

For Women Ready to Build in Real Time

Group Workshops & 1:1 Intensives

- Based on the Process Pro Method™
- Strategy, structure, and support
- Available in private sessions or curated group formats

For Coaches, Creatives, CEOs & Small Businesses

Esyntial Elements Operations Consulting

- Done-for-you workflow and SOP design
- Systems automation and back-end clarity
- For those ready to scale *without* the burnout

For Community & Connection

Stilettos & Strategies Membership + Events

- Where clarity meets sisterhood
- Monthly gatherings, business resources, and growth-stage mentorship
- Judgment-free support, no matter what season you're in

Stay Connected

You are not behind.
   You are not too late.
   You are becoming and I'd be honored to walk with you.

- **Website:** www.nuepps.com
- **Email:** info@nuepps.com
- **Instagram:** @nuepps | @esyntialelements | @stilettosandstrategies
- **Podcast:** *The Process Pro Podcast* www.theprocesspropodcast.com
- **Resources + Merch:** www.nuepps.com/shop

15

Appendix: Frameworks & Visual Models

This appendix includes the original frameworks, diagrams, and visual models developed by the author for *The Process Pro Method™*. These models serve as reference tools to support the principles discussed throughout the book.

The Process Pro Method™ Pyramid

The Process Pro Method™ Pyramid outlines the three layers required for building a sustainable and aligned life and/or business:

1. **Clarity** (Mindset, Movement, Money, Mission)
2. **Systems** (internal and external processes)
3. **Strategy** (the outward execution and growth structure)

This model demonstrates the importance of establishing clarity before building operational or marketing strategy.

The Process Pro Method™

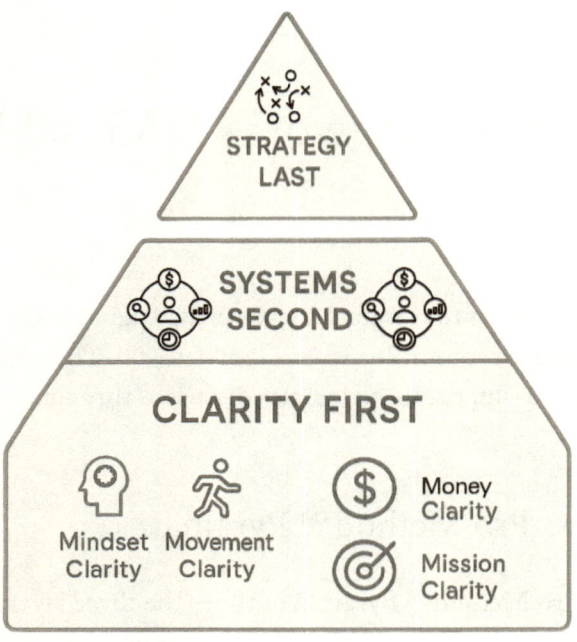

The Process Pro Method™, an original framework by Nu Epps, presents a tiered framework in which strategic clarity emerges from foundational mindset, movement, money, and mission clarity. Visual model created, visualized, and provided by the author, 2025..

The Clarity Journey Staircase™

The Clarity Journey Staircase™ maps the five steps of any clarity process:
Awareness → Audit → Alignment → Activation → Ascension.

This staircase demonstrates the emotional, strategic, and operational progression required for individuals and business owners to achieve sustainable clarity.

The Clarity Journey Staircase™

Clarity isn't found. It's built — one step at a time.

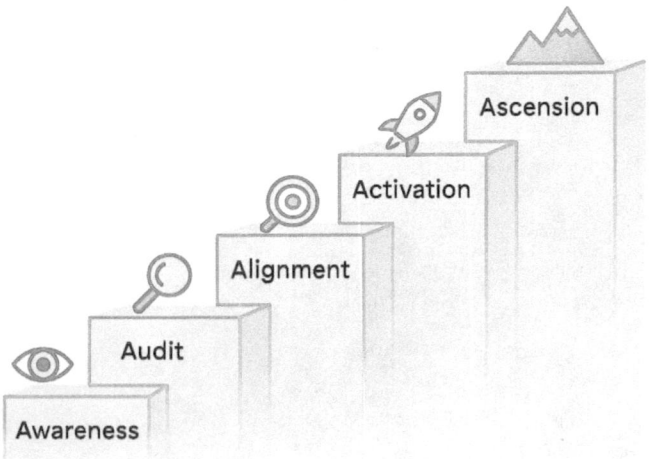

The Clarity Journey Staircase™, an original framework by Nu Epps, offers a sequential model for developing personal or organizational clarity. Visual model created, visualized, and provided by the author, 2025.

The Internal Audit Loop™

The Internal Audit Loop illustrates the continuous cycle of
Reflect → Re-Align → Reinforce → Observe.

This framework is designed to help entrepreneurs maintain internal clarity, emotional consistency, and strategic alignment through structured self-review.

The Internal Audit Loop™

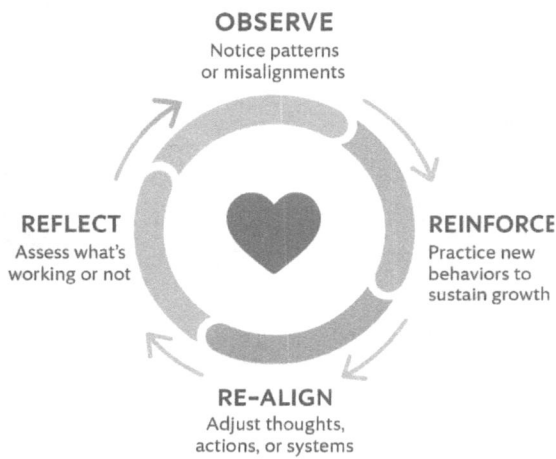

OBSERVE
Notice patterns
or misalignments

REFLECT
Assess what's
working or not

REINFORCE
Practice new
behaviors to
sustain growth

RE-ALIGN
Adjust thoughts,
actions, or systems

When the system breaks, begin within.

The Internal Audit Loop, an original framework by Nu Epps, illustrates a cyclical approach to inner alignment and sustainable growth. Visual model created, visualized, and provided by the author, 2025.

The Feminine Systems Framework™

The Feminine Systems Framework™ integrates relational, intuitive, communal, and nurturing forms of intelligence into business design. The framework honors both structure and softness through four core principles:

- Spiritual Intelligence
- Alluring Delivery
- Maternal Instincts
- Community Relational Magnetism

This model supports feminine affirming leaders in building systems that feel aligned, embodied, and energetically sustainable.

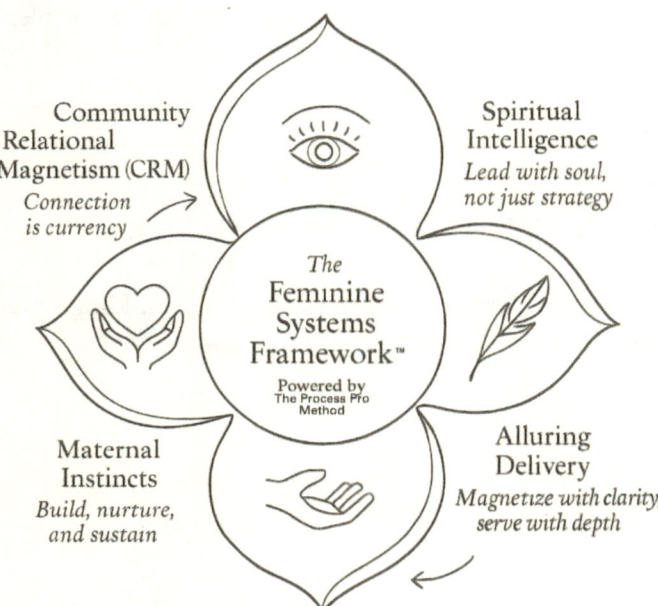

Community Relational Magnetism (CRM)
Connection is currency

Spiritual Intelligence
Lead with soul, not just strategy

The Feminine Systems Framework™
Powered by The Process Pro Method

Maternal Instincts
Build, nurture, and sustain

Alluring Delivery
Magnetize with clarity, serve with depth

This is what it looks like when systems honor softness and strategy at the same time.

The Feminine Systems Framework™, an original framework by Nu Epps, under The Process Pro Method™, proposes a system of leadership and strategy that integrates spiritual intelligence, maternal instincts, intuition, community, and relational intelligence. Visual model created, visualized, and provided by the author, 2025.

The Four Core Systems - Process Pro Method™

Client Flow | Financial Flow | Operations Flow | Marketing Flow

The Four Core Flows represent the foundational systems required for a service-based business to operate efficiently and scale sustainably. These flows illustrate how clients, money, processes, and visibility move through an organization. Each flow outlines bottlenecks, feedback loops, and necessary checkpoints to maintain business stability as well as personal balance rooted in clarity models from the Process Pro Method ™.

The Four Core Business Systems – Process Pro Method™

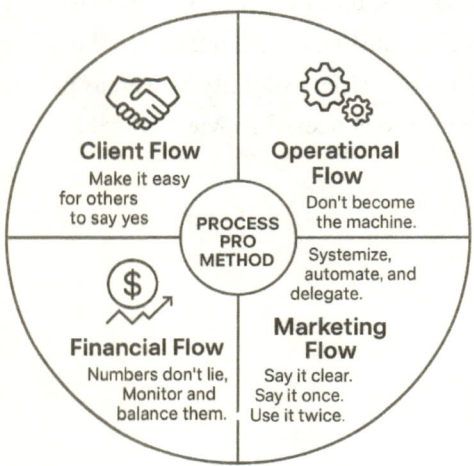

Systems don't remove you from the business. They return you to your genius.

The Four Core Flows—Client Flow, Financial Flow, Operations Flow, and Marketing Flow—were developed by Nu Epps as a foundational systems model within The Process Pro Method™ to place clarity as the foundational center of business systems. Framework created, visualized, and provided by the author, 2025.

16

Notes

1. **The Four Core Flows** – Developed by Nu Epps, this model outlines the movement and interconnection of Client Flow, Financial Flow, Operations Flow, and Marketing Flow in a service-based business. Each flow is a system that requires visibility, structure, and clarity to operate effectively.

2. **The Process Pro Method™ Pyramid** – Created by Nu Epps as the foundational framework of her coaching philosophy, this pyramid emphasizes building businesses "from the bottom up" with Clarity first, Systems second, and Strategy last. It reflects the deep connection between internal alignment and external growth.

3. **The Internal Audit Loop** – A self-assessment tool designed to help entrepreneurs continuously Reflect, Re-Align, Reinforce, and Observe. It represents a cyclical approach to growth, grounded in intentional self-awareness and behavior adjustment.

4. **The Clarity Journey Staircase™** – This staircase framework introduces a five-step process for building clarity: Awareness, Audit, Alignment, Activation, and Ascension. Each step corresponds with an emotional and operational phase in personal and business growth.

5. **The Feminine Systems Framework**™ – A values-based model for honoring feminine intelligence in business systems. Includes: Spiritual Intelligence, Alluring Delivery, Maternal Instincts, and Community Relational Magnetism (CRM). Developed by Nu Epps to blend heart and strategy in sustainable leadership.
6. **General Citations** – While no external frameworks were used directly in the creation of these models, the author acknowledges the influence of classic writing texts that supported the crafting of this book:

- *The Elements of Style* by Strunk & White
- *On Writing: A Memoir of the Craft* by Stephen King
- *The Art of Memoir* by Mary Karr

About the Author

Nu Epps is the founder of Esyntial Elements, a project management and operations consulting firm that helps entrepreneurs build businesses that don't burn them out. She is the creator of the Process Pro Method™, a transformational system designed to help high-capacity women move from chaos to clarity through structure, automation, and strategy.

With more than twenty years of experience in mid-management, entrepreneurship, event production, team leadership, and business operations, Nu blends executive-level insight with lived wisdom. Her voice and vision power *The Process Pro Radio Podcast*, the Stilettos & Strategies™ women's empowerment community, and a growing ecosystem of tools, merch, events, and workshops designed to help visionaries build with intention — not exhaustion.

When she's not working, she's dancing, traveling, attending comedy shows and live music events, or curating unforgettable social experiences for family and friends — living her life with the same joy, structure, and authenticity she helps others create.

You can connect with me on:

🌐 https://nuepps.com

f https://facebook.com/nuepps

www.ingramcontent.com/pod-product-compliance
Lightning Source LLC
Chambersburg PA
CBHW031434120626
46545CB00006B/2398